While every precaution has been taken in the preparation of this book, the publisher assumes no responsibility for errors or omissions, or for damages resulting from the use of the information contained herein.

CHRISTOPHER COLUMBUS: THE UNTOLD STORY OF DISCOVERY AND CONTROVERSY

First edition. August 28, 2024.

ISBN: 979-8227814623

Written by Cassiel E. Nox.

Table of Contents

Christopher Columbus:
The Untold Story of Discovery and Controversy

by: Cassiel E. Nox

1. The Historical Context of Exploration

1.1 Navigating the Age of Discovery

The late 15th century was a time of profound change in Europe, driven by a mix of desires that would soon lead to the Age of Discovery. Economic factors played a vital role as nations across the continent sought new trade routes to spice-rich lands. The allure of wealth from exotic goods was irresistible, prompting monarchs to finance expeditions that could expand their empires and fill their coffers. Countries like Spain and Portugal, eager to outdo one another, created powerful naval forces and invested in advanced shipbuilding techniques. In parallel, the thirst for knowledge ignited a spirit of inquiry, fueled by the Renaissance, which sparked a revival of interest in geography, navigation, and the natural world. This intellectual backdrop encouraged explorers to chart unknown waters and seek distant lands, forever altering the course of history.

Among the luminaries of this era was Christopher Columbus, whose voyages in 1492 would famously connect the Old World and the New. Columbus, driven by ambition and a profound belief that he was on a divine mission, set sail under the Spanish flag, promising to find a westward route to Asia. His first expedition took him across the vast Atlantic, landing in what is now the Bahamas, an encounter that would mark a pivotal moment in human history. Yet Columbus was not alone; figures like Vasco da Gama and Ferdinand Magellan were mapping new sea routes, pushing the boundaries of what was known. Their journeys were fraught with peril, yet the knowledge they brought back opened the floodgates for further exploration, leading to the eventual colonization of large swathes of the globe.

As we delve into this rich tapestry woven by exploration, we must reflect on the broader implications of these voyages. The Age of Discovery was not merely about charting uncharted territories; it also heralded profound consequences for Indigenous populations, who faced cultural upheaval and devastating disease when confronted with

CHRISTOPHER COLUMBUS: THE UNTOLD STORY OF DISCOVERY AND CONTROVERSY

European explorers. We must question how history portrays these interactions. Were they merely a step toward progress, or did they also reveal the darker sides of ambition and conquest? These questions encourage a more nuanced understanding of the past and its lingering effects today. Engaging with primary sources, such as Columbus's writings or the accounts of Indigenous peoples, can provide valuable insights into the motives and experiences of those on both sides of these monumental encounters. Contemplating these narratives enriches our understanding and appreciation of this transformative period.

1.2 European Motivations for Exploration

Throughout the late 15th and early 16th centuries, various economic, political, and religious factors ignited the flames of exploration among European nations. As trade routes to the East became choked and exorbitantly expensive, the allure of new markets provided a powerful incentive for countries like Spain and Portugal to seek alternate pathways. The burgeoning demand for spices, silks, and other exotic goods conducted a symphony that played to the ambition of explorers. With the rise of mercantilism, wealth became synonymous with national power, prompting states to invest in expeditions that promised bountiful returns. This era saw the fusion of individual ambition and national interests as ships braved the unknown, propelled by the promise of profit and a desire to disseminate religious beliefs. The Christian zeal that accompanied many explorations revealed a dual motivation: to secure economic advantage while spreading the teachings of Christianity among so-called 'heathen' populations.

The competition among European powers for wealth and territory heightened the stakes of exploration. Spain and Portugal led the charge, but England, France, and the Netherlands soon joined the race, each driven by national pride and the quest for dominance. The race was not merely about personal glory, but a reflection of national rivalry. As each nation sought to carve out its empire, explorers like Columbus and Magellan became symbols of their countries' ambitions, launching missions fraught with peril. They faced the unpredictable wrath of nature and the fierce competition from rival nations eager to stake their claims. This environment of fierce rivalry fostered a culture of exploration that was both exhilarating and dangerous, with each voyage representing a gamble that could enrich an entire nation or lead to ruin.

The ensuing discoveries ignited a race for colonization and trade to shape global dynamics for centuries.

Considering this complex tapestry woven by economic, political, and religious threads, reflecting on how these motivations affected the relationships between the explorers and the Indigenous societies they encountered is essential. The clash of cultures and the ensuing consequences raise crucial questions about the ethical dimensions of exploration. For instance, how did the European perspective on civilization influence their interactions with native populations? What were the implications of imposing religious beliefs on diverse cultural landscapes? Analyzing these motivations sheds light on the zeal that fueled the Age of Exploration and urges us to examine the foundational aspects of modern global relations born from these early encounters. As we delve deeper into history, remember that understanding the motivations behind such monumental events can enlighten our view of contemporary global ethics and cultural exchange issues.

1.3 The Impact of the Renaissance on Navigation

The Renaissance, a period of cultural rebirth in Europe from the 14th to the 17th centuries, set the stage for remarkable advancements in navigation technology and cartography. This era produced various new instruments that transformed how sailors ventured onto the seas. The astrolabe, which originated in ancient Greece, became more refined, allowing navigators to calculate latitude more accurately. Coupled with improvements in the magnetic compass, these tools ushered in an age where charting a course across uncharted waters became increasingly workable and dependable. Maps also developed, no longer mere depictions of land but detailed representations that included coastlines, tides, and ocean currents. For example, the Italian cartographer Martin Waldseemüller created one of the first maps to name America, illustrating how the thirst for knowledge served scientific and exploratory aspirations. The once-abstract lines of latitude and longitude dominated the practice of navigation, transforming the seas into a vast, navigable highway.

The new knowledge emerging from fields such as science and philosophy profoundly influenced exploration. Thinkers like Copernicus, who proposed that the Earth revolved around the Sun, not only altered perceptions of the universe but also inspired explorers to seek new lands. The philosophical shift from a geocentric worldview to one that acknowledged a broader cosmos encouraged a spirit of inquiry and adventure. These ideas fueled the ambitions of explorers who sought wealth and an understanding of the world's vastness. The creation of nautical charts often included annotations based on the empirical observations of these explorers, thus intertwining science with adventure. Intellectual discussions extended beyond academia's walls. Such dynamics led to expeditions to expand territorial claims and unveil new truths about the Earth and its inhabitants.

As history unfolded, synthesizing advanced navigation technologies and new scientific insights created a powerful impetus for exploration. Appreciating how this context fostered the conditions for discoveries that would shape the modern world is essential. In reflecting on this period, one might consider how knowledge and exploration remain interconnected in contemporary society. How does the spirit of inquiry that marked the Renaissance find expression in today's exploration, be it through space, the depths of the ocean, or unmapped territories of human experience? Understanding these connections enriches our perspective on progress and invites curiosity into exploration in any form.

2. The Man Behind the Voyages

2.1 Early Life in Genoa

The bustling port city of Genoa during the late 15th century was a melting pot of culture, commerce, and adventure. Christopher Columbus was born in 1451 into this vibrant landscape, where the sea was not just a body of water but a pathway to new worlds. A robust maritime spirit marked his early life in Genoa, as the city thrived on trade with various Mediterranean nations. The streets of Genoa were alive with the sounds of merchants negotiating deals, sailors boasting of their journeys, and the scent of salt lingering in the air, all of which captivated young Columbus. Raised in a family of wool weavers, he encountered the struggles and aspirations of those who sought fortune on broader horizons. The family's modest means did not hinder their aspirations, and they often conversed about the tales of daring explorers and their travels across vast oceans. This blend of practical skills and a yearning for adventure influenced Columbus profoundly.

Columbus's education was not strictly formal; instead, it was an amalgamation of experiences and observations. Local sailors and merchants became his teachers, imparting invaluable knowledge about navigation, shipbuilding, and the uncharted waters beyond the Mediterranean. As a teen, Columbus became engrossed in the ambition to explore, fueled by Marco Polo's and other adventurers' stories. His visits to the bustling docks of Genoa were not merely recreational; they were formative as they opened his eyes to a world brimming with opportunity and mystery. Columbus, inspired by his upbringing, had a powerful desire to venture into the unknown, defying societal norms and seeking wealth in far-off lands.

The socioeconomic landscape of Genoa played a pivotal role in Christopher Columbus's ambitions for exploration. The city was a thriving hub for trade, particularly in spices and precious metals, which were in high demand across Europe. This bustling economy generated a competitive spirit among Genoese merchants and sailors. The allure of riches in uncharted lands tempted countless individuals. Seeing the significant wealth amassed through maritime commerce, Columbus became increasingly driven to find alternative routes and lands to elevate his social standing. Economic instability and competition often fueled his desire to pursue exploration for status and prosperity.

The era's political climate was impossible to ignore, with heated debates and enthusiastic protests filling the streets. As European powers, particularly Spain and Portugal, vied for dominance in trade and exploration, Columbus recognized the changing tides of power and the potential opportunities they afforded. His connections in Genoa, particularly with influential figures and the banking community, offered him insights and support to pursue his grand ambitions. The connection between his aspiration to transcend his modest beginnings and the socio-economic trends of his era was clear. Columbus's voyages would not merely be pursuits of land but reflections of the complex interplay between ambition, opportunity, and the insatiable human desire for discovery.

Understanding the formative experiences of Columbus and the socioeconomic factors at play can provide insight into the motivations of countless explorers throughout history. It invites us to think about how our environments shape our ambitions and choices and how the interconnectedness of societies often leads to transformative events. As we reflect on Columbus's early influences, consider your surroundings' role in shaping your aspirations sometimes. Great journeys usually begin in the most unexpected places.

2.2 Influences and Inspirations

A blend of personal mentors and transformative experiences fueled Columbus' ambition to explore the uncharted territories of the world. In the vibrant atmosphere of Genoa's bustling port city, Columbus grew accustomed to the lively shouts of merchants and the rhythmic creaking of ships. His father, Domenico Colombo, a wool weaver, impacted him, teaching him the value of ambition and a thirst for adventure. Columbus often listened to seafarers recount their thrilling tales of distant lands and lucrative trade, igniting a fire in his curious mind. He also met with navigators who traveled to far-off lands, embedding in him a desire to navigate the unknown. His historic journeys, which included sailing along the coasts of Africa and the Canary Islands, further cemented his love for the sea and the lure of discovery, sharpening his resolve to find new trade routes to Asia.

Literature and scientific advancements of the time played a crucial role in shaping Columbus's worldview. Engaging with texts such as Ptolemy's Geography, Columbus became captivated by the concept of a spherical Earth, which contradicted the widespread belief of a flat planet. The ideas of Renaissance thinkers, particularly those advocating exploration and challenging societal norms, enhanced his studies. The writings of Marco Polo, with vivid accounts of the East's riches and wonders, fueled Columbus's imagination about the potential wealth awaiting him in Asia. The unconventional idea of reaching the East by sailing westward influenced him. Columbus's collision of literature and science shaped his unique perspective, driving his voyages and revealing the transition from medieval to exploratory thinking. This blend of personal ambition and intellectual pursuit illustrates how various influences converge to guide individual aspirations.

Considering the complex motivations that drove Columbus, one can reflect on nurturing a curious spirit and the impact of mentorship in pursuing one's passions. For those interested in exploration or personal development, seeking knowledge through varied literature sources, individual connections, or immersive experiences can provide rich insights and inspire daring ventures.

2.3 Columbus as a Navigator and Leader

Christopher Columbus was not just a man with a dream of discovering new worlds; he possessed skills and qualities that made him a remarkable navigator and a compelling leader. His exceptional diligence made him stand out from his peers. Columbus understood the importance of navigation and studying the stars and currents, which he meticulously documented in his journal. He was innovative, employing a blend of traditional knowledge and his observations to direct his ships across uncharted waters. His daring approach included using the latest maritime technology of the time, such as the astrolabe and quadrant, which allowed him to make educated guesses regarding latitude. Columbus's ability to read and interpret maps was legendary; he could visualize his journey before setting sail. This combination of traditional navigation skills and forward-thinking made him a pivotal figure in maritime exploration.

Columbus's leadership style was equally significant in shaping his voyages. He was known for his magnetic charisma, which inspired loyalty from his crew despite their hardships. His decision-making was often bold and decisive, reflecting a contagious confidence. Columbus had a knack for motivating his men, keeping spirits high with tales of glory and riches awaiting them. His method sparked controversy. The dynamics aboard his ships oscillated between exhilaration and fear. Yet, Columbus emerged as a figure of authority who held the crew together, navigating not just through the seas but also the complexities of human emotion and ambition.

CHRISTOPHER COLUMBUS: THE UNTOLD STORY OF DISCOVERY AND CONTROVERSY

3. The Commissioning of the Voyage

3.1 Securing Royal Patronage

Columbus embarked on a long and challenging journey to gain support from the Spanish monarchy for his ambitious plan to find a westward route to Asia. This quest was not merely a matter of presenting a well-thought-out proposal; it required relentless persuasion, careful networking, and a keen understanding of the political tides of the time. Columbus faced an uphill battle, operating in a landscape marked by competing interests, suspicions, and a lack of immediate resources for such an expedition. His hard work resulted in a series of meetings and discussions, leading him to the courts of King Ferdinand and Queen Isabella, who would decide the outcome of his journey. Columbus, drawing upon his skills as a navigator and his knowledge of trade routes, crafted a proposal that sought to emphasize not only the potential riches waiting in the East but also the prowess of Spain on the world stage, which was increasingly important in a Europe characterized by power struggles and territorial conquests.

Engaging with the monarchs required Columbus to navigate the intricate web of political dynamics at the Spanish court. Having just finished the Reconquista, the royal couple had many important matters to address, such as solidifying their rule and ensuring the nobility's loyalty. Understanding this, Columbus tailored his approach to resonate with their vision of a unified and prosperous kingdom. He meticulously highlighted the potential of his voyage to spread Christianity, framing it as a holy mission that would enrich the crown and serve the greater good. Throughout the negotiations, Columbus faced skepticism from advisors who questioned the viability of his plans, yet he remained undeterred. His tenacity shone through as he leveraged every opportunity to advocate for his cause, continually refining his narrative to align with the interests and aspirations of the Spanish crown, leading to their endorsement.

This delicate negotiation dance secured Columbus's fleet and had broader implications, setting the stage for the Age of Exploration. The royal endorsement was not just a stamp of approval; it reflected a central strategic pivot for Spain, marking its entrance onto a global stage that would reshape history—this moment illuminated the interplay of ambition, belief, and politics that characterized Columbus's life and work. For those interested in understanding this period, examining the motivations and responses of both Columbus and the Spanish monarchy offers a glimpse into a larger narrative of exploration driven by competing visions. It is a reminder of how the desires of one individual can collide with the intricate patterns of power and politics, shaping the course of nations.

3.2 Crafting a Bold Plan

Columbus envisioned ambitious objectives for his voyage across the Atlantic, driven by a genuine desire to access the riches of Asia. He imagined establishing trade routes and spreading Christianity among the people he encountered. This dual mission did not just stem from personal ambition; it reflected the era's zeal for exploration, fueled by the promise of wealth and religious expansion. Columbus aimed to sail westward, believing this direction could lead to a faster route to the East Indies. His plan was audacious, for many regarded such a journey as fraught with danger. The allure of golden new worlds filled with precious spices, silks, and jewels tormented him and the Spanish monarchy that financed his expedition. That he could unlock the door to new lands was both promising and dangerous, setting the stage for historic encounters that would alter the course of world history.

Underpinning Columbus's grand design were meticulous scientific calculations and bold assumptions that shaped his plans. He relied heavily on the works of earlier mapmakers and navigators, contributing to his understanding of the world's geometry. His belief in the small circumference of the Earth led him to underestimate the vast distance to Asia, something he reinforced by using inaccurate maps. Columbus also employed celestial navigation techniques, using the North Star and other heavenly bodies to guide his way. His calculations were based on outdated knowledge and his confidence in his theories. This combination of underestimation and miscalculation highlights the complexities of his planning process, revealing the dreamlike ambition intertwined with a dangerous naivety. His risks were monumental, propelled by a vision as bold as flawed.

The story of Columbus's expedition reveals how his dreams and unwavering determination collided with the harsh realities of navigating uncharted waters. By questioning Columbus's decisions and motivations, we can delve deeper into the lessons of exploration beyond the lure of gold. It invites critical thinking about the consequences of such endeavors for the explorers and the Indigenous societies that would encounter them. Engaging with this historical narrative urges us to consider the delicate balance between ambition and responsibility. The complexities of Columbus's voyage remind us that every bold plan carries the weight of unforeseen outcomes, urging us to remain mindful of our aspirations and their impacts.

3.3 Building the Ships: Nina, Pinta, and Santa Maria

Constructed in the late 15th century, Columbus's three ships on his historic voyage, the Nina, Pinta, and Santa Mari, were products of their time, reflecting the era's maritime technology and design philosophies. The Santa Maria, the largest of the trio, was a carrack characterized by her broad beam, topsides, and three masts. Built for cargo and equipped with some heavy artillery, she was suitable for long voyages, though her size would also make her slower compared to the smaller ships. The Nina and Pinta were caravels, smaller and lighter vessels designed for speed and agility. Their slender hulls and lateen sails allowed them to sail closer to the wind, allowing Columbus to navigate the unpredictable waters of the Atlantic Ocean with more excellent dexterity. The choice of these specific designs was critical; they represented a blend of strength and maneuverability, optimized for exploration and potential conflict.

The significance of these ships went well beyond their physical attributes; they were the vessels of exploration that would pave the way for European awareness of the New World. When Columbus set sail in 1492, he embarked on a journey across the ocean and a meaningful path leading to the encounter between two vastly diverse cultures. The comparatively small size of the Nina and Pinta allowed for more straightforward navigation through the treacherous waters, displaying Columbus's understanding of maritime concerns. Each ship played an integral role in the journey that altered the course of history, enabling Columbus to reach the Bahamas and start a new chapter in global interaction. This initial voyage led to the Columbian Exchange, a groundbreaking movement of goods, people, and ideas between the continents, significantly impacting world history. Reflection on these ships invites critical thinking about the events set in motion by

Columbus's undertaking and the profound implications for Indigenous populations, trade, and the development of a global economy.

To delve deeper into the significance of Columbus's ships, consider what attributes were essential for navigating the unknown and how advancements in ship technology influenced exploration during Columbus's time and throughout maritime history. The legacy of Nina, Pinta, and Santa Maria continues to resonate today. Understanding their design choices and significance can foster a greater appreciation for the intricacies of exploration and its lasting effects on our world, encouraging ongoing discussion about maritime history and its vast, untold stories.

CHRISTOPHER COLUMBUS: THE UNTOLD STORY OF DISCOVERY AND CONTROVERSY

4. The First Voyage: Crossing the Atlantic

4.1 Setting Sail: September 1492

As the sun rose over the port of Palos de la Frontera on that fateful day in September 1492, the air buzzed with excitement and apprehension. Christopher Columbus stood on the quayside, his mind racing with dreams of discovery. The ships, the Nina, the Pinta, and the Santa Maria, swayed gently against the tide, their sails billowing like the wings of magnificent birds poised to break free from their earthly bonds. The sight of them stirred not just admiration but legions of doubts and whispers of uncertainty carried by the salty sea breeze. Family and friends gathered to bid farewell, their faces etched with a blend of pride and fear, casting furtive glances at the eager adventurers who dashed towards the ships, their hearts pounding with the promise of the unknown. For Columbus, this was an extraordinary expedition that held profound significance.

The crew, a motley band of sailors, craftsmen, and dreamers, shared Columbus's anticipation, each harboring their visions of what lay ahead. The possibility of wealth and a higher social standing beckoned from afar as they imagined the distant glimmer of gold after years of unnoticed, challenging work. Others clutched hopeful fantasies of encountering uncharted lands filled with friendly natives and untouched beauty, visions pulled from the tales spun by explorers before them. Yet lurking beneath this cloak of optimism was an undercurrent of trepidation. Confessions of fear mingled with prayers to the Virgin Mary for safe passage. Would they find land? Would they survive the hazards of the vast, uncharted ocean, where the horizon blurred and the sun's warmth turned chilling cold? These questions created a tapestry of emotions as each man grappled with the pull of adventure against the familiar call of home.

As they pushed off from the shore, fading echoes of goodbyes mingled with the crash of waves, creating a symphony of human emotion that reverberated in the hearts of those onboard. Columbus stood at the helm, his eyes scanning the endless sea, a mixture of hope and ambition blending with the salty air. The sun rose, painting the land in a breathtaking golden hue, and he could not shake the feeling of anticipation - a new era unfolding, holding the promise of unexplored lands and unfamiliar faces. A shared journey had begun, impacting the world in ways they could scarcely imagine, forever altering the course of history. The winds of change were about to blow, and as they boarded the ship, they could feel the anticipation in the air. As you reflect on this pivotal moment in history, imagine the relentless ambition that propels us to explore the unknown, unveiling hidden horizons in our lives.

4.2 Challenges at Sea: Storms and Mutinies

The journey across the Atlantic was fraught with peril, as the crew of Columbus faced unpredictable weather that could turn calm seas into violent turmoil within moments. Dark clouds loomed ominously on the horizon, often heralding storms that raged with furious intensity. The ship, often barely more than a floating contraption made of wood and canvas, rocked violently on the waves as thunder boomed overhead. Rain fell in relentless sheets, stinging like needles against the sailors' skin. As the long months of travel wore on, many men battled against nature's relentless fury, their resolve pushed to the brink. The fear of capsizing into the abyss was palpable, and their hopes of discovery dimmed amidst the chaos of the stormy seas. Navigating such conditions demanded skill but sheer determination as they struggled against wind gusts that threatened to rip the sails apart and waves that towered like mountains, crashing down with a power that could easily swallow them whole.

Amidst the trials of nature, tensions brewed among the crew, which would eventually bubble over into the open mutiny. Acrimonious disputes over leadership and direction compounded their physical hardships: hunger, fear, and sleeplessness. Columbus, firm in his convictions yet often struggling to unite the men under his command, found himself at odds with crew members who questioned his decisions. Discontent simmered as provisions ran low, and whispers of rebellion circulated in the quiet corners of the ship. The men, weary of the misery and the uncertainty of ever returning home, formed factions, each seeking to challenge the authority of their captain. Their unity frayed, creating an atmosphere ripe for insurrection. The moment came when the mutinous crew confronted Columbus, demanding to turn back, declaring they would not follow him into the unknown without specific assurances of safety and success. A clash of wills unfolded, and the ship's fate hung precariously in the balance, teetering between loyalty to their leader and the desire for survival.

The journey of Columbus not only invited the wrath of the sea but also revealed the frailty of human camaraderie under extreme stress. Each storm that lashed against the ship was a mirror reflecting the turmoil among men, highlighting how quickly hope could transform into despair. The mutinies that erupted were more than mere rebellion; they were the visceral reactions of men grappling with the fear of the unknown and the burden of unfulfilled promises. In examining these challenges, one must consider the resilience required to brave the elements and the intricate interplay of leadership, trust, and desperation. The struggles at sea are a testament to the highs and lows of exploration, the dreams of discovery often paired with the stark reality of human limitations. Understanding these dynamics allows us to appreciate the actual cost of such voyages, inviting more profound reflections on what it means to pursue ambition against formidable odds.

4.3 Landfall in the Bahamas

The moment Christopher Columbus first sighted land was nothing short of euphoric. As his ships approached the edge of the horizon, the soft rays of dawn danced upon the water, illuminating the silhouette of an island. It was October 12, 1492. The crew aboard the Nina, Pinta, and Santa Maria erupted in cheers, their voices mingling with the sound of the waves lapping against the hull. Columbus, cloaked in a mixture of anxiety and hope, stood at the helm, his heart pounding in rhythm with the excitement of his sailors. This moment marked the culmination of their long and arduous journey across the Atlantic and represented an unprecedented milestone in the annals of history. When they reached the shores of what would eventually be named San Salvador in the Bahamas, they were immediately struck by the vivid colors of the wildlife, the softness of the white sandy beaches, and the richness of the surrounding greenery, which stood in stark contrast to the turbulent seas they had crossed. Columbus felt a profound sense of destiny while gazing upon this foreign land, one that would change the course of history forever.

This landfall held profound implications for both Europe and the Indigenous populations of the Americas. For Europe, Columbus's discovery sparked an age of exploration that would lead to conquest, colonization, and a redefinition of power dynamics on a global scale. Nations vied for control over new territories, driven by the promise of wealth, resources, and prestige. Meanwhile, the Indigenous peoples, who had thrived in harmony with their land for centuries, faced a stark and painful reality. Europeans introduced both positive and devastating changes. Disease, violence, and displacement became synonymous with this encounter, as the native populations were ill-prepared for the cultural and physical upheaval that would follow. Columbus often viewed the riches he sought in terms of exploration and discovery. Yet, they came at a catastrophic cost to the lives and cultures of those who had inhabited these islands long before Columbus' fleet arrived. In reflecting upon this, one must consider the gravity of history, the narratives of both the conquerors and the conquered interwoven into a complex tapestry of human experience.

This chapter in history invites critical thought and reflection on the motives and consequences surrounding Columbus's voyages. What does it mean to discover? Is it exploration or invasion? Understanding the multi-faceted impacts of Columbus's landfall in the Bahamas encourages a more nuanced view of history that recognizes the rich cultures of the Indigenous peoples while acknowledging the seismic shifts introduced by European exploration. Reflection on primary accounts, like the journal entries of Columbus himself, reveals a man whose ambitions were grand yet profoundly flawed. This moment, filled with potential, is a foundation for discussions about cultural encounters and their legacies, challenging readers to consider the diverse perspectives involved. The landfall in the Bahamas symbolizes a pivot point in history that invites us to engage with the complexities of the past as we navigate the present and future.

33

5. Encounters with Indigenous Peoples

34

5.1 First Contact: A New World

The morning sun cast a golden hue over the horizon as Christopher Columbus and his weary crew approached the shores of the Bahamas on October 12, 1492. This marked a momentous occasion for Columbus and the Indigenous peoples, who unknowingly stood on the brink of profound change—as the small ships anchored, the crew, filled with a mix of trepidation and excitement, caught their first glimpses of the local inhabitant, tall, influential individuals adorned with simple garments made from woven fibers. Their skin gleamed in the sunlight, bearing the marks of their ancestral land, which had nurtured them for generations.

A strange blend of curiosity and misunderstanding characterized Columbus's first encounters with the Taino people. The Indigenous peoples, intrigued by these peculiar newcomers, approached the ships in canoes crafted from giant trees. They regarded the Europeans with wonder and caution, their eyes wide with the realization that their lives would undergo seismic shifts. Their awe at the sight of the ships and their curiosity about the newcomers' world was palpable. Columbus, intent on documenting his discoveries, recorded their initial reactions in his journal, describing them as gentle and welcoming. His interpretations were influenced by his personal biases and the interests of the Spanish crown, as he endeavored to portray his encounters as remarkable achievements of glory and wealth.

There were intricate layers of perception surrounding these encounters. The Taino people were uncertain about Columbus and his men. They viewed the newcomers not only as strange and awe-inspiring but also as potential threats. The concept of land ownership and territorial boundaries, as understood in European cultures, did not align with Taino practices. This fundamental difference in worldview created the seeds of conflict. Columbus, unknowing of the complexities of these Indigenous societies, interpreted their openness through the lens of European superiority, believing himself to be a bringer of civilization. The absence of immediate hostilities led him to perceive a land of abundance, ripe for the taking, instead of recognizing the rich cultural context of the Taino people's existence.

As these initial interactions unfolded, one cannot ignore their broader implications for both sides. Columbus, buoyed by his belief in destiny, saw the encounters as an opportunity to fulfill a divine mission of spreading Christianity, viewing the Taino as potential converts rather than people with their own spiritual beliefs. Conversely, the Taino were about to undergo profound transformations as they dealt with the imposing foreign culture and the devastating impacts of disease and violence that would ensue from European colonization. Yet, faced with these challenges, the Taino people showed remarkable resilience and adaptability. The initial moments of contact are a poignant reminder that history is frequently a complex tapestry woven from various perspectives, suffering, and misinterpretation.

The analysis of these exchanges invites reflection on how first impressions can lead to lasting consequences, a theme that resonates throughout colonial history. Understanding this pivotal moment encourages thoughtful exploration of historical narratives and the power dynamics inherent in encounters between cultures. What can we learn from Columbus's voyage about the importance of empathy and awareness of diverse perspectives? After carefully thinking about these first meetings, we must acknowledge the significance of history and how it continues to shape our society, impacting the narratives we consciously or unconsciously adopt. The urgency of empathy and understanding in cross-cultural encounters is a lesson we can draw from these historical events.

5.2 Initial Impressions and Misunderstandings

Misunderstandings often arise in encounters between cultures, mainly when expectations and communication styles differ vastly. Following Christopher Columbus' initial encounter with the Indigenous peoples of the Americas in 1492, several cultural disparities arose, leading to mutual confusion and misinterpretations. Columbus, a man driven by ambition and the desire for wealth, arrived with preconceived notions about the world and the people he would encounter. He envisioned a land ripe for exploitation, full of resources to seize for the Spanish crown. His writings convey a sense of entitlement and a lack of understanding of the societies he observed. Columbus and his crew were equally bewildering for the Indigenous peoples, who had rich histories and complex social structures. They faced unfamiliar attire, traditions, and a sense of urgency that differed from their lifestyles. The differences in communication, values, and worldviews created significant gaps in understanding, leading to misinterpretations that would have lasting consequences.

Critical moments during these initial encounters reveal a stark contrast in perspectives. As Columbus claimed the land for Spain, his words were not merely descriptions of the territory discovered; they were declarations of ownership that the natives did not initially comprehend. On one occasion, Columbus recorded in his journal the possibility of enslaving the Indigenous Taino population, displaying a lack of awareness regarding the inherent value of human life. Similarly, upon encountering these newcomers, the Indigenous populations frequently perceived them through their distinct cultural perspectives, resulting in interpretations of their actions and motives that diverged from Columbus's original intentions. A noteworthy incident transpired during a tense confrontation, wherein members of

Columbus's crew apprehended multiple Taino individuals who were functioning as interpreters, introducing a considerable level of intricacy to their relationship. Columbus perceived these actions as justified within the context of his mission, whereas the Taino regarded them as the onset of a tumultuous relationship marked by mistrust and resentment. Collaborative efforts might have fostered a different outcome, but the weight of mutual misinterpretation loomed large, leading to a fracture that echoed through history.

Understanding these initial impressions sets the stage for the profound ramifications that would unfold in the years following Columbus's voyages. Reflecting on the importance of perspective and context in historical events helps illuminate the complexity of human interactions across cultures. Engaging with history requires examining the actions of prominent figures like Columbus and recognizing the narratives of the people affected by such events. This approach encourages a more nuanced appreciation of the past, reminding us there are always multiple sides to a story. Readers should consider how these lessons in communication and understanding apply to contemporary interactions across distinct cultures and contexts, fostering a more compassionate worldview.

5.3 The Taino: Culture and Language

The Taino people were the Indigenous inhabitants of the Caribbean, particularly prominent in the islands of what we now know as Cuba, Hispaniola, Puerto Rico, and Jamaica. They were a remarkable society with rich cultural practices, a distinct social structure, and a deep connection to the land. The Taino lived in villages called Vucayeques, usually near the coast or rivers, allowing them access to abundant resources. Their social structure was hierarchical, with a cacique, or chief, who held political and spiritual authority. A council of nobles supported this chief, showing an established governance system. The Taino economy thrived on agriculture, using techniques like slash-and-burn farming to cultivate cassava, sweet potatoes, and maize while also engaging in fishing and trading. They excelled in crafts, pottery, weaving, and wood carving, creating beautiful and functional objects that reflected their relationship with nature.

Christopher Columbus in 1492 marked a monumental turning point for the Taino people. The first encounters between Columbus, his crew, and the Taino people were characterized by curiosity, trade, and a strong cultural identity, highlighting the Taino's welcoming nature. However, the complexities of this communication went far beyond mere exchanges of goods. Columbus and his men, driven by ambitions of conquest and wealth, misinterpreted the Taino's hospitality as subservience. The Taino people's Arawakan language enhanced communication, but translation caused significant loss. The symbolic wristbands made of beads and shells they offered were tokens of friendship, while the Spanish saw them primarily as curiosities to exploit. As the Taino attempted to make sense of these men who appeared from the ocean, they unknowingly engaged in a cultural exchange that would lead to devastating consequences. The broader implications of Columbus's voyages included the disruption of Taino society, which would soon face violence, enslavement, and a rapid decline because of disease and warfare. This duality of encounter moment ripe with honesty and danger reveals the layered narratives of colonization and the critical milestones in the history of the Caribbean that continue to influence discussions surrounding cultural identity and legacy today.

This exploration of the Taino people, their culture, and the fateful meeting with Columbus deepens our understanding of their history and the complexity of human interaction. When studying these past events, consider the perspectives of the Taino as they engaged with Columbus. Ask yourself how their initial openness contrasts with the destructive actions that followed. Understanding this moment in history can profoundly reflect on cultural exchange and colonial impact, encouraging us to seek genuine respect and understanding in our interactions today.

CHRISTOPHER COLUMBUS: THE UNTOLD STORY OF DISCOVERY AND CONTROVERSY

6. The Quest for Gold and Resources

42

6.1 The Search for Treasure

Columbus' obsession with gold and riches was a driving force behind his expeditions to the New World. He believed vast treasures awaited him just beyond the horizon, driven by tales of lands filled with wealth from earlier explorations. Both the allure of gold and the power potential captivated Columbus. Bursting with excitement, his letters portrayed the shimmering potential of the islands and lands he encountered, presenting a captivating image of a paradise overflowing with abundance. This search for treasure held greater significance than mere personal ambition. He became more determined on each return to Spain - gold would cement his legacy, and riches would vindicate his journeys.

The ramifications of Columbus' treasure hunt extended far beyond his gain, impacting Indigenous societies in profound and often tragic ways. The desire to mine and own gold resulted in the exploitation and oppression of Indigenous communities, causing permanent changes to their cultures and lives. Indigenous peoples, once thriving in their communities, suddenly found themselves caught not only in Columbus's quests but amid aspirations of European empires eager to extract resources. The devastating impact of this unquenchable desire for wealth was severe. Analyzing these events invites essential questions about the cost of exploration and the implications of colonialism. How can we reconcile the heroism of prospecting with the suffering caused to those who lived in these lands? The legacy of Columbus thus becomes complicated, offering lessons on the interplay of ambition, morality, and cultural exchange.

Understanding the search for treasure illustrates the historical motives of individuals like Columbus and the complex effects on societies that often go unrecognized. By delving into primary sources and firsthand accounts, we can appreciate the intricacies of this period and strive for deeper insight into both the adventures of the explorers and the realities faced by the Indigenous peoples.

6.2 Exploitation and Labor: The Role of Enslavement

Columbus's voyages marked a significant turning point in the New World's labor and exploitation history. After landing in the Bahamas in 1492, he came across Indigenous peoples whose lives were on the verge of irreversible change. The immediate imposition of European demands led to systems prioritizing resource extraction over human dignity. Columbus's quest for gold drove him to establish an exploitative framework that included the manipulation and subjugation of native populations. The encomienda system, started by Columbus and refined by his successors, allowed Spanish settlers to claim rights over indigenous labor. Indigenous individuals were compelled to work in mines and on plantations, subjected to a harsh system and enduring brutal conditions. The expectation of labor from Indigenous groups transformed the landscape of the Americas into one of forced servitude, aiming solely to fulfill the insatiable appetite for wealth that European powers demanded.

The human cost of this exploitation was staggering. Indigenous populations, who had once thrived on their lands, faced devastating consequences from European diseases and the oppressive toll of forced labor. Implementing the encomienda system led to decimating entire communities in the affected regions. The initial encounter between Columbus and the Arawak people quickly morphed into a tragedy of enslavement and disease. The accounts from survivors and chroniclers of the time reveal harrowing stories of families torn apart and cultures dismantled. As Europeans sought to convert natives to Christianity and integrate them into a labor force, they often ignored the intrinsic value of these lives, viewing them instead as economic commodities. The ethical ramifications of such exploitation prompt reflection on colonialism and the violence that accompanies it, which still resonates today as one of history's grievous injustices.

Examining these events compels us to confront uncomfortable truths about our past. What does this legacy say about human behavior for power and exploitation? By delving into the narratives of those affected and understanding the broader impacts of Columbus's actions, we gain insight into the history of the Americas and the ongoing discussions about equity, justice, and reparations. Engaging with primary sources, such as diaries of early colonizers or accounts from indigenous voices, can enrich our understanding of this complex history, offering a mosaic of perspectives that challenge us to reconsider the simplistic narratives often presented. However, exploring the profound effects of exploitation in current societies is equally essential, as this is a crucial part of understanding the legacy of Columbus's actions. This past's echoes are not confined to history books; they shape contemporary conversations about heritage and identity.

6.3 The Economic Impact on Europe

The voyages of Christopher Columbus marked a defining moment in European history, propelling economies into an era of unprecedented transformation. When Columbus arrived in the Americas, European economies were primarily agrarian and localized, relying heavily on feudal systems. However, his discoveries opened new avenues for trade and resource acquisition. Having taken the initiative with Columbus's expeditions, Spain tapped into vast wealth from the New World. Precious metals like gold and silver flowed back to Europe, spurring inflation and funding various economic activities. This influx allowed Spain to emerge as a dominant European power and motivated other nations to explore and conquer territories overseas. The transformation didn't just occur in Spain; the entire continent turned its gaze westward. The period saw increased investments in shipping and trade, propelling a shift towards a more commercial economy that included merchants and middle-class citizens, rising in status and influence.

The long-term effects of the Columbian Exchange were vast and complex, intertwining agriculture, demographics, and even culture across continents. This exchange introduced a variety of crops from the Americas, such as potatoes and maize, to Europe, enhancing diets and spurring population growth. As new foods became staples in European diets, agricultural practices shifted, leading to increased productivity. However, this prosperity came at a horrific cost; disease decimated Indigenous populations in the Americas, altering social structures and leading to a brutal system of exploitation. As European nations expanded their empires, they established trade routes that created economic dependencies and reshaped global markets. The impact of the Columbian Exchange laid the foundations of modern capitalism, fostering intercontinental trade that connected disparate parts of the world in ways that had never been seen before. Analyzing these changes prompts us to reflect on the dual nature of Columbus's legacy as a catalyst for economic growth in Europe and a harbinger of cultural destruction and exploitation.

CHRISTOPHER COLUMBUS: THE UNTOLD STORY OF DISCOVERY AND CONTROVERSY

49

7. Subsequent Voyages: Expanding the Empire

7.1 The Second Voyage: Establishing Colonies

In 1493, Christopher Columbus embarked on his second voyage to the New World with a renewed sense of purpose and grander ambitions. Unlike his initial journey, this expedition saw him commanding a much more extensive fleet comprising seventeen ships and approximately 1,200 men. Columbus's primary aim was to establish permanent colonies and secure a foothold in the newly discovered territories, particularly on the island of Hispaniola, which had shown great promise. Upon arrival, his crew faced a vibrant landscape with lush greenery, steep mountains, and Indigenous peoples, who were curious and cautious. The initial interactions displayed considerable potential. Despite the obstacles, Columbus's mission catalyzed monumental changes, establishing settlements that transformed the region and set a precedent for future conquests.

The establishment of colonies during this voyage signified a new chapter in European expansion and ambition. Columbus founded the settlement of La Isabela on the northern coast of Hispaniola, marking one of the first European attempts at establishing a foothold in the Americas. The significance of these colonies extended far beyond mere settlement; they became hubs for trade, agriculture, and the intermingling of cultures, albeit often to the detriment of Indigenous societies. Columbus's actions reflected and contributed to the age of exploration, characterized by a relentless pursuit of wealth and territorial claims. Yet, this expansion came at a heavy price, raising ethical questions about the consequences of colonization. As these new colonies developed, they set the stage for the profound and lasting impact of European influence that would alter the historical trajectory of the Americas, echoing questions about power dynamics, cultural exchange, and human rights that continue to resonate today. Exploring these historical complexities invites a deeper understanding of how these early expeditions shaped a continent and the fabric of global relations.

Reflecting on Columbus's second voyage prompts critical thought about the motivations and outcomes of colonial expansion. How do we reconcile the spirit of adventure and discovery with the often-grim realities of conquest and domination? Engaging with these narratives encourages us to look beyond the romanticized tales of exploration toward a more nuanced understanding of history. The legacies left in the wake of such voyages remind us to consider the broader implications of our actions on the world stage. To fully engage with these narratives, we must strive for a balanced perspective, considering the voices of those affected by these historical events.

7.2 The Third and Fourth Voyages: Further Explorations

Ambition and an unwavering dedication to exploration drove Christopher Columbus during his third and fourth voyages. The primary goal of his third voyage, which began in 1498, was to establish a stronger foothold in the New World. Columbus aimed to find a direct route to the riches of Asia, believing that the islands of the Caribbean were just the steppingstones to a land of golden treasures. His journey took him to the northern coast of South America, where he encountered the Orinoco River in present-day Venezuela. Columbus declared this territory for Spain, further igniting the flames of colonial interest in the Americas. During this voyage, he also encountered Trinidad, a lush island that displayed the diverse landscapes of the Caribbean, reinforcing the notion that this region held untapped riches.

Columbus's discoveries had profound implications. They expanded the European perspective of geography and set in motion the widespread exploration and colonization that would define the following centuries. His encounters with the Indigenous peoples, characterized by curiosity and conflict, would alter the fates of countless communities. He established the first European settlements, creating a path for future expeditions. The ethical implications of colonization sparked significant debates because of the consequences of these encounters.

Columbus's later voyages significantly shaped the Western understanding of the New World. With each journey, he unwrapped a parcel of mysteries embedded in the vast oceans, contributing to the body of knowledge that historians would study. Notably, his fourth voyage in 1502 aimed to find a passage to the Indian Ocean, a quest that led him along the coasts of Central America. This venture, however, was marked by struggle, as he contended with fierce storms and hostility from Indigenous populations. Yet, these trials painted a clearer picture of the challenges accompanying exploration.

Engaging with Columbus's voyages invites us to explore his legacy and the lasting impact of exploration on global history. By examining the nuances of these encounters, one can better appreciate the intricate tapestry of cultures that emerged from this transformative era.

7.3 Legacy of Discovery: Routes and Maps

Analyzing the navigation routes established by Columbus reveals a complex web of interactions and consequences that transformed the landscape of exploration. Columbus's voyages paved alternative paths across the Atlantic and ignited a hunger for exploration that resonated through Europe. His initial route took him from Spain across the open sea into the uncharted waters of what he believed were the Indies. Despite its miscalculations, this fateful journey showed the navigational possibilities that lay beyond the horizon. As a result, subsequent explorers sought to replicate his journey and expand upon his discoveries, motivating expeditions that pushed further into uncharted territories. The corridor Columbus opened became a primary route for trade and colonization, linking Europe to the Americas and catalyzing an era characterized by an elongated interplay between cultures, countries, and continents.

Reflecting on the creation of maps during the age of exploration reveals how crucial these cartographic developments were to the period. Ancient maps were often scarce and imprecise, yet a wealth of new geographical knowledge emerged with Columbus's voyages. Chart-makers incorporated the latest findings into their work, portraying the New World with greater accuracy and detail. The significance of maps extends beyond mere navigation; they served as a knowledge repository, conveying the power and ambition of nations eager to stake a claim in these burgeoning territories. For instance, the T and O maps evolved to highlight what was known of the world, symbolizing both the geography of the time and the prevailing worldview. As explorers ventured outwards, their accounts and the accompanying maps reflected a growing understanding of diverse cultures and ecosystems. This evolution in mapping was more than a response to exploration; it was a catalyst for future exploration itself, sparking curiosity and igniting the imaginations of generations yet to come.

The legacy of Columbus lies not only in his voyages but also in the transformative maps and routes that emerged from his discoveries. Understanding these elements allows today's readers to grasp the profound impact of this era on modern world geography and international relations. Consider how maps continue to shape our understanding of the world; they frame what we know about cultures and histories. Thus, as we explore the past, we can retroactively appreciate the critical role that navigation and cartography play in our ongoing quest for knowledge and connection across the globe.

CHRISTOPHER COLUMBUS: THE UNTOLD STORY OF DISCOVERY AND CONTROVERSY

8. The Controversy of Columbus

8.1 Modern Perspectives on Colonialism

The modern view of Christopher Columbus's actions is closely connected to historical debates. Scholars and historians are now re-evaluating Columbus's legacy, challenging the traditional hero narrative. This reassessment is not just a matter of evaluating past actions; it reflects evolving societal values emphasizing a more nuanced understanding of history. Columbus's expeditions, previously celebrated for their bravery, are now under scrutiny for the harm they caused to Indigenous peoples. The narratives that celebrate his discoveries are increasingly set against a backdrop of colonial violence, exploitation, and cultural erasure. By delving into primary sources, such as Columbus's letters, we find poignant insights into his motivations and mindset, revealing a figure whose ambitions propelled him but also led to unforeseen consequences for the millions affected by his arrival in the Americas.

The debates surrounding colonialism and its long-lasting effects are far from settled. Scholars, activists, and educators continue to discuss the legacies of colonial practices, bringing to light the complexities of power dynamics, cultural exchanges, and systemic inequalities. Some argue that colonialism promotes progress and modernization, while others emphasize the atrocities committed in its name. The dichotomy urges us to question critically: How does the reevaluation of history from marginalized perspectives reshape its importance? How do we honor the experiences and cultures irrevocably changed, often to the detriment of their existence? Engaging with these questions compels us to challenge accepted narratives and consider how colonialism has shaped current global socio-political landscapes. In today's classrooms and public discussions, there is a powerful movement to include diverse perspectives that acknowledge both the achievements and the failures of colonial endeavors, ensuring that the lessons of the past resonate in contemporary dialogues.

As individuals explore the multifaceted implications of colonialism, understanding the perspectives of the Indigenous peoples affected by these historical events is crucial. Engaging with oral histories, cultural artifacts, and contemporary viewpoints allows for a richer narrative beyond traditional Eurocentric histories. This comprehensive approach educates learners and communities about the past and empowers them to think critically about the power structures still present today. By promoting discussions that embody empathy and inclusivity, we dismantle the silos of history that have long divided societal perspectives. People actively seek stories from different voices, share them, and engage in a holistic dialogue about the impact of history on society. This practice deepens individual understanding and cultivates a collective awareness of the past, vital for building a more fair and well-informed future.

8.2 Debates Over the Celebration of Columbus Day

Columbus Day has its roots in the late 18th century, initially commemorated in some parts of the United States as a celebration of Italian-American heritage. When President Franklin D. Roosevelt declared it a national holiday in 1937, it marked a moment of pride for a community facing discrimination. The holiday should honor Christopher Columbus's 1492 voyage, often portrayed as when Europe first connected with the Americas. Yet, the narrative surrounding Columbus is complex and has evolved significantly. Parades and festivities usually accompany the day, fostering community among those celebrating Columbus's legacy. The holiday has stood as a symbol of exploration, discovery, and a specific mythical idea of the New World, which many believe marked the beginning of a new era in history.

However, this celebration is not without controversy, as many argue against honoring a figure whose expeditions led to the colonization and suffering of Indigenous peoples. Critics of Columbus Day point out that his arrival marked the beginning of a violent period of conquest, enslavement, and cultural erasure for Native Americans. They emphasize that celebrating Columbus overlooks the historical realities of colonization and its lasting impacts. The debate has given rise to movements advocating for recognizing Indigenous Peoples' Day as a replacement for Columbus Day, promoting awareness of Native history and resilience. Supporters of this alternative argue it would correct historical narratives and give a voice to those long oppressed. This shifting perspective invites essential questions: How do we reconcile the legacy of exploration with its darker consequences? Should we continue to celebrate those who played significant roles in their time despite the harm they caused? This discourse reflects a broader societal struggle to address historical injustices while honoring the diverse stories that makeup America's identity.

Understanding the complexity of Columbus Day encourages more profound reflection on historical narratives and their implications today. Engaging with different perspectives enhances our understanding of history and promotes empathy for marginalized groups. In discussions about holidays like Columbus Day, it is essential to consider the history of our land and the diverse voices that contribute to its story. Exploring these themes can lead to a more nuanced appreciation of our cultural heritage and inspire communities to create inclusive celebrations that honor all facets of the American experience.

8.3 Critical Histories: Voices from the Dispossessed

The Indigenous perspectives in Columbus and the impact of European colonization reveal a complex and often painful narrative. Columbus' arrival in 1492 started a devastating chain of events for Native peoples, resulting in the loss of their lands, cultures, and identities. When Columbus set foot on the shores of what he called the New World, he did not discover an empty land; instead, he encountered thriving societies rich in traditions and languages. The Taino, for instance, experienced an immediate and brutal transformation as colonizers imposed their will, seeking gold and resources, leading to violence, servitude, and an eventual drastic decline in their population. The suffering of Indigenous communities is frequently overlooked to celebrate Columbus as a heroic explorer.

In examining these indigenous voices, the narrative of history gains depth and nuance. The oral traditions, written records, and personal stories of Native peoples challenge dominant historical accounts that glorify European exploration. They offer an essential re-examination of Columbus's legacy, highlighting themes of resilience, resistance, and the ongoing impact of colonization that reverberates through contemporary society. For example, community leaders today continue to address past injustices while advocating for cultural revitalization and recognizing Indigenous rights. These perspectives encourage readers to reflect on the broader impact of his journeys, prompting us to consider matters of historical remembrance, power dynamics, and whose opinions hold precedence. This engagement with dissenting voices not only enriches our understanding of the past but also informs our present, reminding us that history is not just a series of events but a tapestry of human experiences, struggles, and triumphs.

64

9. Columbus's Legacy in Spain and the Americas

65

9.1 Spain's Transformation: From Empire to Exploration

Analyzing the profound changes within Spain following Columbus's voyages reveals a nation on the brink of transformation. Columbus' flagship, the Santa Mari, became a symbol of adventure and curiosity, igniting the imaginations of countless Europeans. Filled with hopes of new riches and lands, his sails swept across the Atlantic Ocean in 1492, billowing with determination. Upon his return, Columbus brought tales of unexplored lands teeming with abundant resources. This discovery sent ripples through every facet of Spanish society. The monarchy, previously focused on consolidating power within the Iberian Peninsula, gazed outward. The Catholic Monarchs, Ferdinand and Isabella, saw the potential to expand their influence, converting wealth gathered from newfound lands into tangible power. Merchants and nobility funded voyages themselves, sparking a competitive spirit that would characterize this new age of exploration. As tales of gold and exotic peoples reached the ears of the populace, cities like Seville and Cadiz became thriving centers of trade, bustling with activity and vibrant cultures converging from across the globe.

As exploration spurred Spain's rise as a global power, it did so with an almost unimaginable speed and intensity. The influx of gold and silver from the New World significantly enriched the Spanish crown, fueling military campaigns and establishing Spain as a preeminent force in Europe. The newfound wealth transformed the social fabric of Spanish society: new jobs emerged in trade and navigation, while a burgeoning class of merchants and explorers challenged the earlier socio-economic hierarchies. Spanish ships dominated the seas, creating an empire spanned vast oceans and territories. This momentum led to establishing colonial enterprises in the Americas, drastically altering global trade routes and interactions between diverse cultures. However, while Spanish wealth and power surged, it also bred conflict and tension, both within the kingdom and abroad. Spain's expansion was not without its controversies, as Indigenous populations faced exploitation and violence. The balance between ambition and ethical considerations regarding colonization became a topic of heated debate. As Spain forged ahead, the exploration it embraced was a double-edged sword, prompting questions about the consequences of empire-building and the actual cost of ambition.

Viewing this complex era through today's lens offers valuable insights. One reflection that resonates is the transformation of identity and culture in the wake of Columbus's voyages. It is a powerful reminder of how exploration can reshape societies in unforeseen ways. As students of history, understanding the narratives that propel nations is crucial. Encouraging critical reflection draws parallels between the motivations that propelled explorers in the past and those that drive contemporary quests for discovery. The lessons from Spain's transition from empire to a global power remain relevant; they prompt us to question how we engage with new worlds today through travel, trade, or cultural exchange.

9.2 Columbus in American Memory

Columbus has been remembered in American history and culture as a daring explorer whose voyages opened the New World to European colonization. Initially hailed for his interactions with the Americas, his reputation has adapted to shifting societal values and historical viewpoints. Columbus became a symbol of progress and exploration in the 19th century, shaping American cultural identity. Schools educated children about his adventures, creating a narrative celebrating his bravery and ingenuity. The multitude of statues and the national recognition of Columbus Day solidified his esteemed reputation as an American hero. This respected image disintegrated in the second half of the 20th century, when historians and the public reassessed the impact of his expeditions. With critical examinations of Indigenous peoples' suffering and colonization emerging, the romanticized vision of Columbus clashed with the harsh realities of history. The once-unquestioned legacy of Columbus became entangled in the broader conversation about race, colonialism, and historical responsibility, challenging Americans to reconsider whom they choose to honor and why.

Various emotions and reactions arise in contemporary society as it tries to navigate the complexities of Columbus' legacy. Some perceive Columbus as a courageous explorer deserving of celebration, while others contend his actions inflicted immense suffering on Indigenous populations. This dichotomy reveals the difficulty inherent in reconciling a historical figure's accomplishments with the profound impacts of their actions. Activists and Indigenous groups have called for a reexamination of public monuments, advocating for the replacement of Columbus statues with memorials honoring those who resisted colonization or celebrating Indigenous cultures. This evolving discussion invites individuals to reflect on their beliefs about history and memory. Does Columbus deserve recognition as a pioneer or as the catalyst for centuries of oppression? These questions are deeply personal and often evoke enthusiastic debate, underscoring the pervasive influence of Columbus in American dialogue. As we continue to confront the legacies of historical figures, a more thoughtful engagement with history is not just desirable; it is our responsibility to push us toward a more responsible and engaged understanding of our past.

Understanding the full scope of Columbus's impact can be enlightening. This exploration invites everyone to dive deeper into colonial history and consider how we assign value to historical figures. Reading diverse narratives, especially those from Indigenous perspectives, can enrich and broaden our comprehension of America's past, offering a more complete picture of our history.

9.3 Statues and Public Perception

Monuments dedicated to Christopher Columbus are potent symbols representing a moment in history, cultural heritage, and identity complexities. The towering statues, often positioned in prominent public squares, have sparked intense debates. Supporters view these monuments as tributes to an explorer who opened the Americas to European civilization. Critics argue they serve as reminders of colonization, exploitation, and the devastating consequences suffered by Indigenous peoples. In cities like Baltimore, New York, and Los Angeles, rallies to protect these statues have collided with movements advocating for their removal, reflecting deep societal divisions. The controversies surrounding these monuments have led to vandalism, removal, and even public disdain, prompting questions about who claims history and what narratives are honored in our public spaces.

Public perception of Christopher Columbus has evolved drastically over the centuries. Columbus was praised as a fearless adventurer who faced the unknown, becoming a heroic figure in the years that followed his expeditions. Children learned of his daring journeys across the ocean, often accompanied by tales of triumph and discovery. However, as historical scholarship progressed, narratives shifted. The darker aspects of Columbus's expeditions emerged: the enslavement of Indigenous populations, the spread of disease, and the subsequent colonization that decimated entire cultures. Today, classroom discussions, media, and community forums reveal a transition from outright admiration to critical examination. This shift urges society to revisit historical narratives with nuance and complexity, encouraging individuals to engage with challenging questions about legacy, morality, and interpreting history, stimulating intellectual curiosity and growth.

As the debate over monuments continues, it becomes increasingly important to grasp the multi-faceted nature of historical figures.

CHRISTOPHER COLUMBUS: THE UNTOLD STORY OF DISCOVERY AND CONTROVERSY

Understanding Columbus's impact requires us to acknowledge his achievements and the profound suffering accompanying his voyages. This nuanced understanding fosters deeper conversations about how communities remember their past and encourages a more inclusive approach to history. These discussions also prompt readers to reflect on the narratives that shape their communities. Consider the monuments in your area, what they celebrate, and whose stories they leave untold. Engaging with these questions can lead to a richer understanding of history and its ongoing influence on shaping present and future identities.

72

10. The Role of Religion in Columbus's Journeys

10.1 The Catholic Monarchs and Their Influence

The rule of the Catholic Monarchs, Ferdinand of Aragon and Isabella of Castile, was significantly shaped by their religious beliefs, supporting Christopher Columbus's expeditions. They genuinely believed in spreading Christianity, not for political gain. The recent unification of Spain under their rule, achieved through the Reconquista, a campaign to reclaim the Iberian Peninsula from Muslim control, further fueled their religious fervor. This victory reinforced their belief that they would promote Catholicism globally. In Columbus, they saw an opportunity for wealth, territory, and the long-awaited expansion of their faith. They pledged their support for his voyage across the Atlantic, driven by the vision of new lands where they could establish Christianity in the name of Spain, aligning their imperial ambitions with their spiritual mission.

The implications of this deep-seated religious fervor went far beyond the simple pursuit of exploration. It marked the beginning of an era characterized by a blend of faith and expansion that would profoundly alter the world's landscape. Columbus' expeditions had a broader purpose beyond the exploration of new lands. This mindset set a precedent for future explorers, who often justify their colonization efforts as a divine mandate. The attempt to convert Indigenous peoples usually led to the profound disruption of their cultural and spiritual fabric, causing extensive devastation to entire civilizations. We cannot ignore such a significant legacy. The interplay of faith and empire-building raises questions about morality, governance, and the true nature of progress, compelling us to ponder the cost of such fervent ambitions as we explore the consequences of their actions.

Stories from this era, including the fraught encounters between European explorers and Indigenous communities, serve as critical touchstones for understanding our world today. They remind us that as we seek to explore new frontiers, whether physical, intellectual, or spiritual, we must consider the implications of our pursuits. Seeking adventure and knowledge comes with responsibilities that history has often laid bare, urging modern explorers to proceed with a more reflective lens.

10.2 Columbus's Personal Faith

The religious convictions of Columbus played a significant role in shaping his identity and impacted his remarkable expeditions across unknown seas. Born into a devout Christian family, he fervently embraced Christianity when faith was pivotal in everyday life. His letters and journals frequently reveal a deep-seated ambition to spread Christianity to new lands, which he viewed as a divine mission ordained by God. Columbus believed in the predetermined nature of his voyages, finding solace and resilience in this conviction as he navigated uncharted waters and encountered unfriendly situations in the Americas. His faith fueled his determination to face the unknown, viewing each star in the night sky not just as a navigational aid but as a divine guide, steering him toward fulfilling what he perceived as his rightful purpose.

Exploring the intricate relationship between faith and discovery in Columbus's narrative unveils a complex portrait of the man and his motivations. Through his writings, Columbus often articulated his experiences as a quest for wealth and a sacred pilgrimage. He believed that by discovering new lands, he was uncovering a path destined by God to fulfill biblical prophecies, as he frequently referenced bringing the Gospel to Indigenous populations. This perspective invites readers to ponder the intertwined nature of faith, exploration, and the consequences of cultural encounters. When he claimed the land for the Spanish crown, he declared it a dominion for Christ, reflecting a worldview where faith justified conquest. This crucial intersection prompts critical reflection on whether Columbus's devout Christian heritage catalyzed remarkable discoveries and profound ethical dilemmas. This examination continues to resonate in discussions about his legacy today.

Columbus's faith encourages an examination of his reasons and the broader consequences of his encounters with native populations. The intensity of his convictions raises essential questions about the impact of one person's quest for exploration. How did his actions reflect his faith, and what were the consequences for the people living in the lands he tried to conquer? This dynamic interplay between conviction and global impact prompts deeper contemplation on how faith shapes history and influences actions reverberating across time and culture. Understanding Columbus's faith provides rich material for further study, inviting us to question not just the outcomes of his voyages but also the very nature of belief itself and its power to inspire exploration and exploitation.

10.3 Conversion Efforts in the New World

Columbus's voyages in the late 15th century marked the beginning of significant changes for the Indigenous peoples of the Americas, including the spread of Christianity. Columbus and his crew landed on various islands and encountered richly diverse cultures and spiritual beliefs. Driven partly by his devout faith, Columbus often viewed these encounters through a lens of religious duty. He believed it was essential to convert the native populations to Christianity, seeing their conversion to save souls. Historical records, including Columbus's journals, reveal his genuine desire to evangelize the Indigenous people as he sought to establish a Christian empire in the New World. Reports from his interactions exhibit a mix of admiration and condescension. Columbus referred to the natives with a sense of bewilderment, yet he also saw them as potential converts who needed guidance in his eyes. His encounters, such as those with the Taino people, resulted in cultural exchanges and attempts to introduce them to the Christian faith, albeit often misguidedly presented.

The ethical implications of religious conversion during this period are profoundly complex and invite critical examination. While the spread of Christianity brought certain cultural exchanges, it also frequently involved coercion and violence. The motives behind these efforts often included a desire for territorial expansion rather than purely altruistic concerns for the souls of the Indigenous peoples. Imposing European religious beliefs usually resulted in the eradication of Indigenous traditions and identities, inflicting lasting harm across successive generations. A considerable proportion of Indigenous groups were forced to renounce their traditional spiritual rituals and embrace the faith imposed on them by their colonizers. Examining these actions creates an opportunity to reflect on the consequences of colonization, not just in terms of cultural loss but also moral responsibility. With Columbus as a focal point, one can question the legitimacy of conversion under such circumstances, highlighting the tension between the noble aspirations of bringing faith and the grim realities of conquest. Understanding this historical context is crucial, as it allows for a more nuanced conversation about the legacies of those who sought to evangelize Indigenous populations amidst a backdrop of exploitation and oppression.

Examining the ethical considerations of conversion during Columbus's era prompts vital discussions about historical remembrance and the lessons we can learn. Those delving into this period might consider how the narratives of colonizers and the colonized differ and how those variations can influence contemporary societal views on faith, identity, and reconciliation. As we study Columbus's legacy, reflecting on the balance between cultural exchange and erasure can provide insights into modern discussions surrounding globalization, cultural sensitivity, and preserving Indigenous rights.

80

11. Primary Sources: Voices from the Era

11.1 Journal Entries of Christopher Columbus

Examining Columbus's journal as a primary source of his experiences is crucial in revealing a vivid narrative of exploration filled with wonder, challenges, and profound encounters. His writings, crafted in the early 15th century, paint a rich tapestry of his voyages across the Atlantic. Each entry gives a window into his daily life aboard the ships, detailing everything from the unpredictable weather to the anxiety of navigating uncharted waters. Columbus's accounts of the sea went beyond simple observations, revealing a profound attachment to the immensity of the ocean. He often mused about the stars guiding him and the winds that could thwart or embrace his journey. The journal also chronicles his encounters with Indigenous peoples, noting their appearances, customs, and languages. Through these reflections, we can see the physical landscapes he discovered and the emotional and psychological landscapes he traversed during his journeys.

Discussing how these writings provide insight into his thoughts and motivations invites us to understand Columbus as an explorer and a complex figure driven by ambition and a sense of purpose. His entries reveal a man deeply motivated by the promise of glory and riches but also one who grappled with uncertainty and fear. His language often conveyed excitement and trepidation, illustrating his desire to achieve fame, serve the Spanish Crown, and further the spread of Christianity. Yet, his writings also reflect a sense of naivety about the lands he encountered and the people he met, displaying a limited understanding of their cultures and the consequences his actions would unleash. By delving into Columbus's journal, readers can ponder critical questions about the legacy of his voyages: What drove him to undertake such dangerous journeys? How did his interactions with various people shape the course of history? By engaging with these texts, one can gain a nuanced appreciation of Columbus' motivations while grappling with his discoveries' profound impacts on the world.

Reflect upon the historical significance of Columbus's words and their contextual influence. His journal serves as a personal account and a vital record that encourages us to reflect on the narratives of exploration and conquest. This primary source allows us to question the nature of discovery and its moral implications. As modern readers, we can analyze these writings, engaging with the text and its meaning on multiple levels, prompting thoughtful discussions about legacy, responsibility, and our interpretations of history.

11.2 Accounts from Crew Members

While Christopher Columbus is often celebrated as the bold navigator who discovered the New World, the voices of his crew members offer a nuanced perspective that adds depth to our understanding of these historic voyages. Those who sailed with him recorded their sea experiences, attitudes, and the realities of life on board. For instance, his logbooks contain entries from Columbus and other crew members whose observations illuminate the dangers, hardships, and ethical dilemmas the expedition posed. For example, a sailor named Pedro de Medina recorded the crew's emotions when they first caught sight of land. The crew's enthusiasm turned into fear and moral questioning as his words stirred a blend of wonder and apprehension.

These accounts hold significant importance in piecing together the crew's collective experience. They challenge the myth of Columbus as a solitary hero, revealing instead a tapestry of human emotions, aspirations, and conflicts. Crew narratives expose the brutal onboard realities, such as the grueling labor, relentless anxieties tied to navigation, and the precarious nature of long sea voyages. The crew's voices are also crucial in understanding the interactions with Indigenous peoples, as they express astonishment, confusion, and even guilt in the face of their encounters. By engaging with these lesser-heard perspectives, we gain a fuller picture of the implications of Columbus's decisions, allowing us to reflect critically on the consequences that still resonate today. The stories shared by his crew members are not just footnotes in history but essential narratives that compel us to reconsider what we learn about exploration, conquest, and colonization.

Reading these personal accounts cultivates a more profound empathy and encourages us to ask questions beyond the merely factual. What motivated these sailors to embark on such perilous journeys? How did their allegiances and morals shift during their encounters with new lands and peoples? By delving into the crew's accounts, we honor diverse perspectives and foster an environment for critical discussion about history's more complex layers. Engaging with primary sources, whether through logs or letters, brings us closer to the lived experiences of those who sailed, urging us to consider the broader ramifications of these historical actions both at sea and on land.

11.3 Indigenous Narratives and Perspectives

Indigenous accounts of Columbus's arrival in the Americas provide a vital lens through which to understand the profound impact of his voyages on Native communities. These narratives, often captured in oral traditions, writings, and historical records, reflect not just the immediate disruptions caused by contact but also the resilience and agency of Indigenous peoples. Tribes such as the Tai no, the Arawak, and others recounted experiences laden with emotion, complexity, and depth. Their stories reveal a spectrum of responses from initial curiosity and hospitality to fear, resistance, and eventual confrontation with the realities of colonization. These narratives are not merely historical artifacts; they offer perspectives steeped in human experiences, joys, losses, and transformations, enriching our understanding of this pivotal historical moment.

Understanding these Indigenous narratives is essential for fostering a more balanced view of history. They question the frequently biased narratives of exploration that celebrate Columbus while disregarding the perspectives of those who bore the consequences of his actions. Incorporating these accounts unveils a more inclusive narrative that acknowledges the prosperous civilizations predating European interaction alongside the explorations and conquests. Gaining a thorough understanding of this historical context compels us to evaluate critically the repercussions of colonialism and acknowledge the enduring presence of vibrant Indigenous cultures. Such narratives provide essential questions for modern readers: How do we define exploration versus invasion? What responsibilities do we have in acknowledging these histories? Engaging with Indigenous perspectives broadens our understanding and fosters empathy and respect for the diverse tapestry of human experiences. Every tale is a reminder that history is not a mere record, but a chorus of voices seeking to make themselves heard.

88

12. The Impact of Columbus's Voyages on Indigenous Societies

12.1 Changes in Demographics and Social Structures

The demographic shifts following European contact with Indigenous peoples were profound and often devastating. As explorers like Columbus made their journey across the Atlantic, they inadvertently introduced various changes that would alter the landscape of the Americas forever. Europeans marked the beginning of a tragic decline in the Indigenous population because of a combination of diseases, violent encounters, and displacement. Before Columbus's voyages, the Indigenous populations were diverse, each community with its traditions, languages, and ways of life. However, introducing smallpox, measles, and influenza, to which the native peoples had no immunity, led to catastrophic mortality rates. According to estimates, these diseases affect up to 90% of specific populations. The loss resulted in a significant disruption of the demographic balance, devastating the cultural diversity and community leadership structures in place for centuries. The devastating impact of colonization extended beyond the loss of lives and encompassed the shattering of social connections and long-established support systems that held great significance for various Indigenous cultures.

The social structures in Indigenous societies shifted because of increasing external pressures from European settlers. Once flourishing and intricate, Indigenous communities encountered contemporary power structures imposed by Europeans, often neglecting local traditions and governance. The establishment of trade relations initially brought opportunities for certain tribes, but usually resulted in the loss of their sovereignty and autonomy. The exchange of goods and services led to shifting alliances, as Indigenous groups aligned themselves with Europeans against rival tribes, resulting in changes to established relationships and cultural practices. The need to allocate land and scarce resources prompted the reorganization of societal roles in several tribes. European settlers replaced traditional leaders or influenced them with their ideals. The creation of new social norms often stemmed from the need to survive in an increasingly hostile environment. Indigenous populations' resilience in adapting to these changes is a testament to their strength, yet it also highlights the painful transformations forced upon them.

Understanding these demographic and social shifts invites a more profound reflection on the historical consequences of European exploration. Consider how the narratives of triumph and discovery often overshadow the brutal reality of colonization for Indigenous peoples. What legacies remain today because of these changes? Exploring these questions can enhance one's appreciation of Indigenous cultures' richness and the complex tapestry of history that shaped modern societies.

12.2 The Introduction of European Diseases

When Europeans first arrived in the Americas, they carried with them not just their goods and aspirations but also a suite of diseases that would prove catastrophic for the Indigenous populations. Smallpox, influenza, and measles illnesses that had become common in Europe were foreign to the native inhabitants. Lacking immunity, entire communities faced unimaginable devastation. Sometimes, mortality rates soared as high as 90 percent in certain tribes. These diseases swept through vibrant societies that had thrived for centuries, often leaving behind ghost towns where once bustling communities existed. The physical landscapes echoed the silence of those lost to disease, leading to a permanent alteration in the demographic makeup of the Americas. The scars from the experience remained on the land and in the cultural memories and identities of those who survived.

As the spread of European diseases altered the indigenous landscape, so did it shape the course of colonization. The weakened states of native populations made them more vulnerable to European conquest. Colonizers seized this opportunity, often justifying their violent actions by pointing to the decimation caused by disease. Resistance to colonization, while still fierce, was frequently undermined by the rapid decline in the strength of Indigenous groups ravaged by illness. Native leaders who might have organized powerful alliances found their ranks thinned, making it difficult to mount effective opposition to European encroachment. This interplay between disease and colonization reveals a complex layer to the exploration narrative, underscoring the tragedy of ambition meeting vulnerability. This prompts a crucial contemplation on the repercussions of these expeditions, compelling us to ponder how factors beyond mere intentions frequently influence history through unforeseen biological exchanges that can permanently shape civilizations.

Understanding the interplay of disease and colonization is crucial. How have these historical events influenced contemporary discussions of health and cultural interactions? Exploring these connections may provide insights into current global issues and remind us of cultures' resilience in the face of overwhelming change.

12.3 Resistance and Adaptation by Indigenous Peoples

Indigenous societies have shown remarkable resilience in the face of colonization, facing profound disruptions yet continually adapting. When European explorers like Christopher Columbus first set foot in the Americas, they encountered diverse cultures rich in traditions, languages, and social structures. These encounters often led to devastating consequences, including violence, disease, and a loss of land. Yet, against these overwhelming odds, Indigenous communities displayed incredible tenacity. They preserved their languages, traditions, and connection to the land while creatively navigating the challenges. Families and clans united in specific regions to resist colonization, collaborating through resource and knowledge sharing. Stories of Indigenous leaders rising to prominence during these turbulent times highlight the strength and resolve of these communities. Figures like Tecumseh and Sitting Bull emerged as symbols of resistance, embodying the spirit of their people and leading efforts to reclaim autonomy, provide for their communities, and resist forced assimilation.

Strategies of resistance often intertwined with adaptation, revealing the complex ways Indigenous peoples responded to their changing realities. During colonization, communities developed distinct forms of expression that helped shape their identity. Through establishing trade networks, Indigenous peoples exchanged goods and ideas with European settlers while subtly maintaining their cultural identity. Others embraced innovative agricultural practices, blending traditional techniques with colonizers' lessons. For instance, the establishment of the Matis culture in Canada illustrates a unique fusion of Indigenous and European traditions, highlighting how people can create entirely new identities from the ashes of colonization. Spiritual practices persisted in varying forms as a balm for communities to heal from trauma and keep cultural narratives alive. Oral histories, storytelling, and traditional ceremonies persisted through generations, ensuring the continuity of cultural memory despite external pressures. A vibrant tapestry of resistance emerges that celebrates the indomitable spirit of Indigenous societies, prompting reflections on the complexities of adaptation in the face of systemic change.

13. Columbus in Popular Culture

13.1 Literature and Film Depictions

Christopher Columbus, a figure of enduring fascination, has been a central character in stories and movies for centuries. Often depicted as the intrepid explorer who discovered the Americas, his portrayal in literature and film has helped to shape a diverse and dynamic narrative of historical representation. Ancient accounts, such as Washington Irving's 1828 biography, cast Columbus as a romantic hero, accentuating his resolve and visionary spirit. While celebrating Columbus's triumphs, Irving's narrative overlooked the darker aspects of his voyages, such as their impact on Indigenous populations.

In contrast, more modern depictions often take a critical stance, reflecting a growing awareness of the consequences of Columbus's expeditions. Films like '1492: Conquest of Paradise' attempted to grapple with the complexities of Columbus's legacy, highlighting both his ambition and the devastating effects of European colonization. The portrayal of Columbus in various works highlights the shifting narratives influenced by cultural perspectives and historical context. This has led to a landscape where literature and film become battlegrounds for competing interpretations of Columbus's actions.

The depiction of Columbus carries significant implications for public understanding of him and the events linked to his expeditions. Romanticized portrayals contribute to a simplified and often glorified image of colonial exploration, leading to the view of Columbus as a national hero. This narrative fosters a sense of pride, particularly in nations descended from European settlers while obscuring the realities faced by Indigenous peoples. As audiences absorb these narratives, their understanding of history becomes shaped by a lens that may overlook the suffering and displacement caused by European actions.

As you delve into literature and films that depict Columbus, it is crucial to consider how these narratives shape your understanding of history. By critically engaging with these works, you can take an active role in deepening your comprehension of Columbus's actions and the broader story of exploration and its consequences. This critical engagement empowers you to form a more nuanced and accurate understanding of history.

13.2 Myths and Misconceptions

The history of Christopher Columbus is obscured by various myths, making it difficult to determine the true impact of his voyages. One of the most persistent misconceptions is that Columbus arrived in the Americas. The reality is much more nuanced than this statement suggests, as it overlooks the significant contributions and enduring presence of Indigenous communities on the land. The notion that Columbus was universally celebrated as a hero upon his return is misleading. Despite achieving fame, his treatment of Native Americans and the harsh realities of his leadership generated substantial controversy in his lifetime. The image of Columbus as an adventurous, noble explorer obscures the darker aspects of his legacy, including enslavement and violence against Indigenous populations. When studied through primary sources like his journals and accounts from his contemporaries, Columbus's voyages reveal moral ambiguities often ignored in popular depictions.

Understanding these misconceptions is crucial for grasping the broader context of the Age of Exploration. They remind us how history can be shaped by perception and bias. When we take the time to peel back the layers of myth, we reveal the complexities of cultural interactions and the consequences of colonization. This reflective analysis helps us see Columbus not merely as a figure from the past but as a catalyst for change and conflict, prompting modern dialogues about the legacies of colonialism. The implications of these misunderstandings influence how we teach history, shaping the narratives shared in classrooms and public discourse. Engaging with these myths invites critical thinking and encourages a more nuanced view of history. It also underscores the power of historical narratives to inspire or distort and the weight of our responsibility in accurately representing diverse perspectives to portray our shared past. Stressing the need to recognize the myths surrounding Columbus is a decisive step in fostering a more informed society.

When you encounter a historical narrative, consider the untold or oversimplified stories that may be present. Histories can be complex, with each layer uncovering distinct truths influencing our comprehension. Interact with sources, challenge existing narratives, and reveal the voices often excluded from the story. The active approach entails more than just learning; it requires taking responsibility for deepening your understanding of history and forming meaningful connections with the diverse experiences that make up our human journey.

13.3 Educational Approaches to Teaching His Legacy

The current educational methods for teaching Columbus' legacy in schools prioritize a comprehensive approach to historical comprehension. Educators face growing pressure to integrate diverse source materials, including primary documents, Indigenous perspectives, and contemporary assessments. This alteration holds immense importance, as it allows students to have a more nuanced interaction with history. For instance, rather than focusing solely on Columbus as a solitary hero or pioneer, educators highlight the complex interactions between Columbus and the native populations he encountered. This includes examining the voyages through the lens of cultural exchange, economic motivations, and the subsequent impact on Indigenous societies. Class discussions often center on these themes, fostering an environment where students can share their thoughts and insights. Projects that involve research into both Columbus's achievements and the views of those affected by his actions encourage deep and critical analytical skills.

The role of critical thinking in historical education is of paramount importance. Students must go beyond surface-level comprehension and analyze potentially biased narratives to comprehend Columbus' impact fully. Educators aim to cultivate a curiosity for inquiry, urging students to contemplate questions like: What were the consequences of Columbus' voyages? How did these voyages change the course of history for Europe and the Americas? Through debates and analytical writing assignments, students learn to evaluate different perspectives and develop their informed viewpoints. This method enhances their understanding of Columbus and equips them with the critical skills needed for interpreting history. As they analyze diverse narratives, they become more aware of their biases and the importance of considering multiple sides of a story. Educators can further this dialogue by integrating interdisciplinary approaches that connect history with literature, social studies, and ethics, encouraging a broader understanding of our shared past.

104

14. Reflection on Historical Narratives

14.1 The Importance of Multiple Perspectives

The narration of history is one-sided. However, the truth is much more intricate. When we delve into historical events, understanding them from multiple perspectives reveals a richer narrative. Take Christopher Columbus, for example. Traditional accounts celebrate his voyages as daring feats of exploration, lauding his courage and ambition. However, these stories frequently gloss over the consequences of his actions on Indigenous populations. By examining history through the eyes of those who lived it, both the European explorers and the native peoples, we encounter a tapestry of experiences that invites us to consider the broader implications of one man's journey and the varying narratives that emerged from it.

The practice of inclusivity when recounting history enhances our understanding. Providing a platform for marginalized voices allows for a more nuanced portrayal of the past. As an example, it is essential to acknowledge that the Indigenous peoples of the Americas had well-developed cultures and histories predating European contact. The narratives of conquest and colonization have often eclipsed these narratives. Including diverse sources, including oral histories, cultural artifacts, and contemporary analyzes, fosters a more holistic comprehension. This raises pivotal questions: What motivations drove Columbus, and how did his actions resonate across historical contexts? What can we learn from the experiences of those affected by his voyages? By inviting these diverse viewpoints into our historical discourse, we honor the complexities of our past and enrich our interpretation of the world today.

Exploring history through various perspectives is an academic exercise and a powerful tool for fostering empathy and understanding. Engaging with stories from multiple angles, we can better grasp the intricate dynamics of power, culture, and identity that shape our world. This approach prompts us to assess critically the narratives we encounter, enriching our appreciation for the rich, often tumultuous interplay of human experiences. By consciously incorporating a range of voices and perspectives, we cultivate a more profound, more informed worldview that recognizes the importance of every individual's story within the broader context of history.

14.2 Revising History: The Role of Historians

Historians often seek to uncover the truth hidden within the layers of time. Established narratives can undergo substantial changes with fresh evidence emerging or exploring different perspectives. This process involves reexamining artifacts, documents, and even the motives behind actions taken by historical figures. For instance, the voyages of Christopher Columbus have been reassessed through various lenses. Scholars dive into logs, letters, and chronicles that illuminate not only Columbus's ambitions but also the consequences of his adventures on Indigenous populations. Historians uncover a multifaceted narrative by examining these sources, shedding light on different perspectives, and amplifying the often-overlooked voices. Societies grow and change, and through the lens of time, historians are skilled at weaving new interpretations that resonate with contemporary values and understandings, enabling us to grasp history as a living tapestry.

Yet, the journey of reinterpreting history is fraught with challenges. Historians must navigate the murky waters of established narratives while confronting deeply ingrained societal beliefs. This craft can evoke enthusiastic debates, especially around topics that touch on national identity or cultural pride. Historians may encounter resistance from individuals who perceive their cultural heritage to be under scrutiny when they challenge conventional perspectives. Making historical interpretations accessible and relatable without oversimplifying complex issues is no small feat. Balancing the scales of evidence with the emotional weight of memories and communal narratives requires a deft touch and a commitment to integrity. How does one honor the past while shedding light on uncomfortable truths? This is a delicate dance that historians must master, one that invites the public to engage in meaningful dialogues about where we come from and what it means for our future. In this context, critical thinking becomes a vital tool for historians and society reflecting on their work.

Understanding historians' role in revising narratives encourages us to question and explore history actively. Primary sources, eyewitness accounts, and the writings of the time serve as breadcrumbs, guiding us to a clearer understanding of the events that shaped our world for individuals seeking to delve deeper into historical narratives, taking part in local history groups, visit museums, or exploring archives can be profoundly enlightening. These experiences allow one to connect directly with the past, prompting moments of reflection and discussion. The history we learn is not just a static record, but a dynamic conversation that evolves as we reassess our understanding of ourselves and our society.

14.3 The Future of Historical Inquiry

Speculating on the future of historical inquiry reveals a landscape shaped by curiosity, innovation, and the relentless pursuit of understanding. Just as the annals of history have evolved, so will the methods we employ to study them. Likely, scholars will increasingly turn to interdisciplinary approaches, intertwining history with fields like sociology, anthropology, and even psychology. This convergence could lead to richer narratives that explore who did what and when and the deeper motivations and societal contexts behind these actions. The more we look back, the more we realize the need for a nuanced understanding, showing that future historians should consider the complexity of experiences to enrich historical narratives.

Technology will shape history by influencing how historians access, analyze, and present primary sources. The digitization of documents, images, and artifacts facilitates unprecedented access to materials once confined to vaults and archives. Resources like online databases and digitized libraries broaden the scope of inquiry, empowering researchers to uncover lesser-known events or obscure figures who previously lay in the shadow of more significant historical movements. Artificial intelligence and machine learning algorithms could assist historians in sifting through vast amounts of data, uncovering patterns and connections that might otherwise go unnoticed. As students, educators, and curious minds navigate this future, developing critical skills for evaluating sources in an age saturated with information will become crucial. A thoughtful engagement with these technologies can enhance our exploration of history, driving home the essential truth that while the tools may change, the need for rigorous analysis and ethical inquiry remains steadfast.

The landscape of historical inquiry is undeniably evolving. Engaging with this dynamic field invites individuals to cultivate a critical perspective, prompting questions about how we frame our narratives and understand our world. By incorporating many voices and experiences, historical narratives gain vibrancy and depth. Those interested in exploring this future should dive into digital resources available today, using online forums, virtual museums, and educational platforms that challenge conventional narratives and expand our understanding. These tools are not merely accessories to studying history but integral to fostering an informed and reflective society.

15. Lessons from Columbus's Journey

15.1 Ethical Considerations in Exploration

Exploration has long been a narrative of human curiosity, courage, and ambition, but it also carries profound ethical implications. The actions of explorers like Christopher Columbus, whose voyages started significant cultural exchanges but also triggered devastating consequences for Indigenous populations, invite us to reflect on the responsibilities that come with exploration. Columbus's expeditions opened new worlds for Europeans, yet they also heralded the onset of colonization, resulting in countless individuals' exploitation and suffering. An ethical examination of exploration demands we ask challenging questions: To whom do we owe accountability when our pursuit of knowledge and discovery undermines the lives and cultures of others? Columbus's encounters with the Taino people highlight a complicated blend of curiosity and violence. His initial encounters, marked by wonder, soon morphed into cruelty as his quest for gold and glory overshadowed humane values.

Columbus's legacy looms large over the conversation about future exploration. In a larger historical context, the emphasis on exploration often detracted from the appreciation of the vibrant cultures and breathtaking natural landscapes that his journeys epitomize. The ongoing debate about celebrating or condemning Columbus raises questions that resonate today. Are modern explorers learning from the past, or do they repeat the same patterns of ignoring the ethical implications of their pursuits? As we contemplate expeditions to uncharted territories or contemporary digital frontiers, such as space exploration, we must consider the impact of our actions on both the environment and the lives of people who inhabit those areas. We must assess carefully the individuals entrusted with documenting the history of exploration, emphasizing amplifying the voices of those marginalized who have suffered the consequences of explorers' endeavors. Our commitment lies in ensuring proper recognition and respect for these voices. Introspection and dialogue are essential for nurturing a responsible approach to exploration that honors both the drive to discover and the duty to uphold ethical standards.

It is crucial to engage with history in a way that sparks discussions about our collective ethical responsibilities as explorers, whether on land, in the ocean, or even in the digital realm. Educators, writers, and learners alike can benefit from pondering the implications of past actions while fostering a culture of awareness and respect for all cultures and histories. Employing this strategy deepens our understanding and urges us to contemplate ethical approaches to exploration. As we venture into the future, let each exploration be a bridge to understanding rather than a gateway to exploitation, urging us to reflect on the legacies we wish to create.

15.2 Understanding Cultural Collisions

The voyages of Christopher Columbus in the late 15th century represented a remarkable exploration of new lands and the start of profound cultural collisions that forever changed the course of history. When Columbus first landed on the shores of the Bahamas in 1492, he encountered the Taino people, whose lives, customs, and beliefs were utterly foreign to him. The first meeting was a mix of curiosity and miscommunication, with Tai not being hospitable and eager to engage with the newcomers by offering gifts and help. Columbus, however, viewed them through the lens of European superiority, often interpreting their kindness as a sign of weakness. As the encounters progressed, this misunderstanding laid the groundwork for exploitation, violence, and the tragic aftermath that ensued, including the decimation of Indigenous populations through disease, enslavement, and warfare.

The repercussions of these cultural collisions have manifested throughout history, influencing the modern world significantly and often troublingly. The interactions started by Columbus set off a wave of European colonization that reshaped the Americas, established new trade routes, and led to the transatlantic slave trade. This era not only resulted in economic exploitation but also the forced cultural assimilation of Indigenous peoples, as European languages, religions, and customs supplanted native traditions. Today, the legacies of these encounters are still apparent as we navigate the complex realities of multicultural societies, global interactions, and the ongoing challenges faced by Indigenous communities seeking recognition and rights. These historical collisions encourage us to reflect on how we understand cultural differences and the importance of emphasizing respect and empathy in our increasingly interconnected world.

As we delve into these aspects of history, it raises critical questions: How does our perception of historical figures like Columbus shape our understanding of cultural collisions? Can we learn from past mistakes to foster a more inclusive future? Engaging with primary sources, such as Columbus's journals and accounts from Indigenous people, can provide deeper insights and a more nuanced view of these remarkable events. Embracing this exploration enriches our knowledge and aligns us to appreciate the diverse tapestry of cultures that have emerged from these historical encounters.

15.3 Relevance of Columbus Today

Columbus's journeys, which encapsulated the age of exploration, still echo in conversations about globalization and identity. His voyages changed the interconnectedness of the world. The exchange of goods, cultures, and ideas that began in his time laid the groundwork for the global economy we experience today. As ships traversed oceans to connect continents for trade, similarly, the internet and modern transportation have now shrunk the world, leading to an unprecedented flow of information and cultural exchange. Columbus symbolizes humanity's hope and ambition to discover the unknown in these discussions. Despite this, the voices of the Indigenous peoples, who experienced the consequences and disturbances, are frequently disregarded in the narratives of his expeditions. Thus, Columbus remains a figure that invites deep reflection; he is both a catalyst for change and a representative of colonialism, compelling us to confront the complexities of legacy in an increasingly globalized context.

A critical examination of Columbus's impact invites us to analyze the outcomes of his voyages and the motives behind them. One should question the price of ambition in pursuing wealth and the discovery title. Columbus marked the beginning of a colonial era that brought suffering, violence, and exploitation to Indigenous populations across the Americas. This reflection prompts us to engage thoughtfully with history. Recognizing Columbus's significance in opening transatlantic routes while acknowledging the devastating impact of colonization is crucial. Such reflections resonate in contemporary discussions, from appropriating cultural identities to the debates on globalization's impact on local customs. As we navigate this complex past, engaging with diverse perspectives allows us to appreciate better how identities and history intertwine, reminding us that history is not a single narrative but a tapestry of interconnected stories.

CHRISTOPHER COLUMBUS: THE UNTOLD STORY OF DISCOVERY AND CONTROVERSY

One practical approach to examining Columbus's legacy is to seek literature and resources that present varying perspectives on his voyages. This can foster a more nuanced understanding of the historical context and its implications. Discussing this legacy can also encourage critical thinking about how history influences modern societal structures. Reflection on these topics can be enlightening, prompting deeper inquiry into the consequences of exploration and colonization that continue to shape our world today.

References

Books and Articles

1. Fernández-Armesto, F. (1991). Columbus. Oxford University Press.
2. Sale, K. (1990). The Conquest of Paradise: Christopher Columbus and the Columbian Legacy. Knopf.
3. Todorov, T. (1984). The Conquest of America: The Question of the Other. University of Oklahoma Press.
4. Mann, C. C. (2005). 1491: New Revelations of the Americas Before Columbus. Knopf.
5. Hulme, P., & Whitehead, N. L. (Eds.). (1992). Wild Majesty: Encounters with Caribs from Columbus to the Present Day. Oxford University Press.

Primary Sources

1. Columbus, C. (1492-1504). The Diario of Christopher Columbus's First Voyage to America, 1492-1493. Edited and translated by O. L. Thacher, 1903.
2. Medina, P. de. (1545). Arte de navegar. Venice: Joannes Baptistae Pedrezano.

Indigenous Narratives and Perspectives

1. Keegan, W. F. (1989). The People Who Discovered Columbus: The Prehistory of the Bahamas. University Press of Florida.
2. Wilson, S. M. (1997). The Indigenous People of the Caribbean. University Press of Florida.

Journals and Articles

1. Rabasa, J. (1993). "Allegories of the Atlas." Representations, 41, 92-112.
2. Kupperman, K. O. (1993). "Fear of Hot Climates in the Anglo-American Colonial Experience." The William and Mary Quarterly, 50(2), 213-240.

Online Resources

1. National Humanities Center. (n.d.). Columbus and the Taíno. Retrieved from http://nationalhumanitiescenter.org/pds/amerbegin/contact/text1/columbustaino.pdf
2. Smithsonian Institution. (n.d.). Columbus and the Age of Discovery. Retrieved from https://www.si.edu/spotlight/columbus